Praise for Lightsey Darst

"[Darst] has the unique ability to express motion with words." **—MPR**

"This is a vital poetry of the Deep South ripe with bones, blood, and bogs . . . a harrowing stew of lust, dusk, and summer." **—The New York Times**

"Darst's intimacy here is masterful: whether it is love, lust, pregnancy, or words." **—The Millions**

"For Darst, to remember is to claim ownership of one's pain and, by extension, one's humanity." **—Publishers Weekly**

"As they carve their way through this markedly contemporary landscape, Darst's readers will likely have trouble separating the dreams, desires, and fears the speaker expresses from their own—the text of these poems is everything you might catch yourself thinking, and everything you might hope someone else could share with you." **—The Arkansas International**

"One of [*Thousands'*] strengths is how Darst weaves quotations, dates, and places into her work, making attributions in the margins. It allows the reader to feel both intimately involved as an observer, but also, somehow, present. . . . This is a collection in which all readers will recognize something, if in nothing else then in the humanity of the poet herself." **—The Paris Review**

"[*Thousands*] has an intimacy about it that speaks to the tenderness inside the reader. . . . Don't be surprised if there's a catch in your throat when you read." **—Signature Reads**

"Simultaneously vulnerable and self-assured, Darst's verse will have you clamoring for everything she's ever written." **—Bustle**

"Dear fear, dear darkness, dear misunderstandings, dear life, dear lost-in-myself, I am no longer afraid of you. Now I have this book. I have Lightsey Darst's amazing and ecstatic meditation on being a person in the world, I have these poems to guide me, I have her bravery and wild mind, I have her spells and wisdom, I have these incredible poems to carry with me wherever I go." **—Matthew Dickman**

"Bluegrass and teen lust, the sequels to horror films and the modernist fragment, perennial myth and murder mystery, all erupt into Lightsey Darst's serious poems. . . . Playing hooky, playing dead, playing 'an instrument built from her body,' Darst is playing with fire: her verse lights up the night sky." **—Stephanie Burt**

"DANCE is to *The Divine Comedy* as Darst is to Dante: heretical. . . . Anarchic, critical, and brilliant, built of many voices, these brave poems give to our radical uncertainty and certain complicity testimony that doesn't diminish their power to unsettle us. This is an ambitious, ethical book—'nothing else / does justice to this year.'" **—Brian Teare**

"[*DANCE*] is the book I hadn't known I'd been waiting for—until I read it, riveted. Anchored in a shifting history, propelled by a phosphorescent phrasing that subtly startles, it's a book whose structure echoes Dante while its tone invokes the gothic. The whole demonstrates just how the present is constructed of every past moment, and how those moments still inhabit it, never silent. But it's above all her handling of language; as rich as the fox furs, comets, and botanical detail she brings to her pages, Darst's sculpted syntax and charged vocabulary keep the text moving with an uncanny depth to their pacing. It will keep you up at night." **—Cole Swensen**

"*Find the Girl* is a book of poems as urgent as its title. . . . Here we have an important new poetic voice, one that fully earns Louis Zukofsky's observation that, in poetry, 'Each word itself is an arrangement / The story must exist in each word or it cannot go on.' Lightsey Darst has internalized this, practiced it, perfected it, and brought it to us in this incredible collection. She has done something truly new."
—Laura Kasischke

"We should not lie about life. *Find the Girl,* in its violent intricacies unearthed by the hand of a poet dutiful to the women and girls long lost from poetry, knows this. . . . *Find the Girl* is an important, ravaging debut." **—Katie Ford**

the heiress / ghost acres

the heiress / ghost acres

Lightsey Darst

COFFEE HOUSE PRESS
Minneapolis
2023

Coffee House Press books are available to the trade through our primary distributor, Consortium Book Sales & Distribution, cbsd.com or (800) 283-3572. For personal orders, catalogs, or other information, write to info@coffeehousepress.org.

Coffee House Press is a nonprofit literary publishing house. Support from private foundations, corporate giving programs, government programs, and generous individuals helps make the publication of our books possible. We gratefully acknowledge their support in detail in the back of this book.

LIBRARY OF CONGRESS CATALOGING-IN-PUBLICATION DATA

Names: Darst, Lightsey, author.
Title: The heiress, ghost acres / Lightsey Darst.
Other titles: Ghost acres
Description: Minneapolis : Coffee House Press, 2023.
Identifiers: LCCN 2022040236 (print) | LCCN 2022040237 (ebook) | ISBN
   9781566896733 (paperback) | ISBN 9781566896740 (epub)
Subjects: LCGFT: Poetry.
Classification: LCC PS3604.A79 H45 2023 (print) | LCC PS3604.A79 (ebook)
   | DDC 811/.6—dc23/eng/20220826
LC record available at https://lccn.loc.gov/2022040236
LC ebook record available at https://lccn.loc.gov/2022040237

The artwork on the front cover is *Ohne Titel, 1964* by Eva Hesse, reproduced with permission of the Estate of Eva Hesse, courtesy of Hauser & Wirth. Image supplied by Kunst Museum Winterthur; donated by Beat Wolfer, Marianne Wolfer, and Silvia Largo-Wolfer, 2000. © SIK-ISEA, Zürich (Jean-Pierre Kuhn)

PRINTED IN THE UNITED STATES OF AMERICA

30 29 28 27 26 25 24 23   1 2 3 4 5 6 7 8

table of contents

THE HEIRESS

This is no time for self-defense.
My father seemed to think it was an important skill.
My daughter's sick again, she stumbles
arms out desperate for me.
I'll nurse her though we've been weaning,
two months pass and I'd nurse her,
now it's July and what would I give to nurse her again and be
one of two who are as happy as god can make them.
Oh what can I give them
that I never had? Not money, earth, myself—
there's less and less of all three. Not safety. What then?

This book begins with a body in need.
And being it. Being me.
Free the future from the past. Free the present
from the distant future. Free the
past to be young again, Rebecca standing in her garden
whatever garden, whatever land—what she wanted
perched in her hand and follow that
to the present it makes, her happiness, truth, her justice.
But why live in a dream.
This demand of emotional accuracy while I'm
figuring out where to get another $500.
I'm going to go quit everything. Don't call back.

I want to appear, walk out a real person
from my life. *ETERNAL DRAMA*
I write above times for tours of my son's school and when
do I get to work out and what will I make
for Thanksgiving and when
will a center arise from these pieces?

This year of realizations.
They fall out of the walls like ancient bones,
thaw from the glacier's husk like the matted fur
of the first woman. I go along picking them up,
a beachcomber after a hurricane.
I pocket drowned women's wedding rings.
Pull the real from the rhythmic waste of the past.
I will do incredible things.
A decade I tossed into the sea.
Is this my life's work? My life. A work.
My life as a plastic. My mold.
I am a forest, a focus, fierce.
Work until ink-soaked paper blackens pants.

A girl evangelist shows up at your door thinking
she knows a truth that's never been thought.
Get down what you think you know
as a place to start.
She walks away, gleam of suffering on her skin.
I know that walk, that sackcloth sway.
She's someone from your hometown, someone who
maybe never had a substantial conversation with a Black woman.
It's not all about the future. It changed the world.
By "it" I mean my children, of course.
So I looked for the speaker and found myself in the mirror,
turned myself in and spent the reward money, loosed
a map of the cosmos and there was I. Pink dust. Pink
meaning hot, a beginning; background
radiation, sign of a one-time explosion.
So it's time to put it together.
Without a second thought, without understanding,
someone's head crowning through your thighs.
She's coming on like rain.

INFERNAL SELVES

What comes first? The names of trees.
Sycamore, red maple, tulip poplar, I always heard *tulapoplar*.
The road in forks into bramble and branch.
Old washing machine, rusted refrigerator—
it's been a hundred years since I've been here,
so tell me: does the white oak
still stand by the dead lake, its folds of bark
hanging like an old woman's labia?
Does the bee tree thrum by the dry lake bed?
The house across the field, the light went out
the first year we lived there.

တာ

I—narrowest of selves, a door open a crack.
We the family, the living, *they* the past.
Only time lies between them and us,
time and the willingness to change. Only the willingness
separates us from them and them from
you, a room in which to stage this séance.

တာ

Know your history.
Know you come from a stone crop and go back there.
Bole of the maple tree your mother planted may survive you.

Their home has become ruin, become a biodynamic farm,
become a Walmart with sweet blood dripping from
the joists, blood that tastes of you.

In this land they did wrong
and though it's burned into the ground
so easy to follow their trace in the fields
we must not go the same way.

On the census of 1830
in Jefferson County in the Florida territory,
the nameless wife of one Hugh Duncan,
age 20–29, born in North Carolina, she swarmed in her season.
The *X* of her who lived burns down my blood.
Hold the shroud three inches from your face and say,
"I'm not dead,
I'm Rebecca and I'm not dead yet."

ᴚ

Everyone's tragedy is a family tragedy.
"This world is not my home," said everyone
in my mother's family, my mother's father's family,
people from Surry County, Virginia,
kin to Eldridge Maddera, to Powhatan Sledge,
who on the 1850 slave schedule
reported nine slaves by sex and age, not name, and so it went
all across Surry County, Virginia,
in 1850 and 1860 when the slave schedules were taken
along with the names of your white children,
children who grow up to say,
"This world is not my home."

ᴚ

Am trying to write
from the record
but where it touches the pain
of another
my paper crumbles.

They
are a distraction,
humans in a record of monstrosity
where you are the monster. Write the monster.

ᴚ

Coast of fire—
you leapt, you never saw it again.
You burn the woods where you mean to live,
kill the people who come out.

Later, on a farm in Carolina,
acid of ownership gnaws you.
Keeping people, you are not a person now.
Your children crowd around your void,
you teach them to be void too.

☙

Scan of an infernal document
does nothing to the screen.

"Oh they were ordinary people"
"Did what ordinary people do"
"Ordinary, then, to own a few"

"Knowing that it is appointed for all men to die
Nothing doubting but at the general resurrection
I shall receive the same again
and as touching such worldly
Estate wherewith it hath pleased God
to bless me I give devise and dispose"

Who is the man hoping for heaven while he parcels out a family with his pigs?
My fifth great-grandfather

You're a channel: a shoal of ghosts swims through you to the sea.

☙

I was born in Mecklenburg County in 1862,
seemed we'd lived there a long time.
A hundred years is a long time, it's one life long.

My mother, she touched the hand
of a woman who married a Confederate soldier.
It was 1950 in Surry, Virginia,
it was August in the field of the past,
when Mama touched great-grandmother Valeria's hand.
A hundred years is three rows of graves,
enough to pack a church, enough
to make a massacre
this little congregation
dirt to staunch the blood.

୬

Her son was shot and buried in a shallow grave.
"Take me to him." Who are we
in this story—the murderer or the murdered Union spy,
the man who owned the land where the mother
pulls her son from unpacked earth, his purple
jaw, untended wound on his chest
flower where his heart was.
She pulls him from his shallow grave,
turning the beloved body as if to wake him from sleep.
He will never be older, she will become as old as forever.
Were we both or only the murderer
Surely we were the murderer but were we also the mother
shaking his shoulder, brushing leaves
and dirt from his face
His wounds multiply, we cannot hold
We were the man who owned the land
torn and watered with her tears
One of many graves, one of many mothers
We owned the field that never gave flower again
we worked that field with its strange patch of luxuriant green.

୬

But give me one self I can feel.

Today when I find my way to the page
a sinkhole. Drain the sinkhole and find

Rebecca, born 1815 or 1809 or 1820,
mother of four children or two or none,
married twice or three times, born
Rebecca Duncan, Rebekeh Dunkin, born Rebecca.
Cannot read or write, born North Carolina
and never been back, Rebecca,
daughter or sister and wife or mother
to men who fought and killed for land,
Rebecca, died 1871 in the place I was born, died
from her name and buried no place, buried
in the trench of the past, Rebecca.

Choosing at every crossing the nameless branch
I find my way back to you.

တ

                                    Florida, 1838 (Second Seminole War)

This is wild country but we are wilder people
Who knew how to get at the heartmeat of a saw palmetto

lies dust and teeth. With seam-ripper and garden claw
with fire and a magnifying glass

Someone's ash sown in Rebecca's field.
Her house a broom never could sweep clean.

တ

Are you my mother
        I was never a mother

Are you my sister
        I was his sister
Are you my home
        Home? A din of walls that lean, picked clean
I've been looking for my aunt could you be her
        Describe her
I saw her once or twice a beautiful woman but turned the other way
        Often I looked like that
What was your name
        Rebecca
But that was every white woman's name
        Rebecca

∽

A body travels a narrow bridge that leads
only to the future.
Dearly have I bought this future
dear the banks of iris beside it.
To build a meadow
from the marrow,
a place later they will say they saw fireflies.
In the crotch of this maple tree to hollow out
oblivion, a place to go when we all die.
A heaven! to stack on the back
of a buried person
neck broke, jawbone
tilts back upper from lower as if to
drink the whole weather.

∽

Are you my good mother
        I did what they needed
Did you do good in this place I came from
        I forget what I did
Did you breed up goodness for me
        You know the answer to that

∽

"Rebecca": to tie, to bind.
They tell a story that ends in you.

If you don't want a white nation you're not what they worked for.
But standing with your white children on your land, you are what they killed for.

∽

What did you feel when they went off to war
        I felt good
Why because they were gone or because you believed in the cause
        I felt good because I was alive
        Why do you ask me these questions
I need a place to begin
        You're grown aren't you
I need a place to rest my head
        Girl, you can lay your head down here if you like
        in this dead lap, if you're that tired
        you can lay your head

∽

I can't deal with my ancestors, they're dead and buried.
It's myself I need to deal with.
My mother sends me my grandmother's hand mirror.
So I can see myself the way the dead see me?
Or the way they see themselves.

∽

Nothing I did was written down
though I made a generation.
I am the stillness and its many arms,
dark licking the spine of the record.

Did I want her—more than wind,
more than stars in winter.
Did I bear her. Nearer than heart
Did I lay her in the dirt

What in this December
might blossom from a cruel clearing.
Daffodil marks a gate, lilac a front door,
this sway of land my grave.

Good-bye to the earth, I loved you.
That spring of rain and selfishness,
any flower in my hair. I don't regret a thing. I'm surviving,
for if I don't survive, girl, how will you?

༚

Are you the mother of my bones
            I am the mother of your bones
Are you my mother
            Are you my daughter

༚

Herself feeds a garden, Venus looking-glass
so it's not a garden but a patch of weeds.
I always loved, she loved
those purple climbers—vetch, and henbit

I know you, who are you
walking among my rib bones
breathing in my bone dust
dust of thunderhead, dead

in name only.

Edith Lorraine Duncan, 1913–2010

I smooth her dawn-down hair, tell her I love her.
Light the house, fix the broken cup.
No, it was my grandmother's cup that was broken—
the cup her grandmother gave her, and her father broke it.
This is a hundred years ago. My heart
is a hundred years old—her cup shatters on the kitchen floor . . .
And I'm remembering now how after my grandmother died
my mother found a box that said
To keep and cry over, and it was about her mama
and her daddy (I think that's how she called them),
and I found a marmalade jar full of ends of string,
and we found a cigar box covered in decals
with the picture of an otter on the top,
like a saint. My girl ripped a book
to hear it tear. But I don't want it permanent—
I get the tape to show her things can be fixed.

EDUCATION OF AN HEIRESS

1

Everywhere men dressed like white supremacists lean.
Clean-cut, close-mouthed, are they Nazis or do they just
listen to their mothers. A basic white boy sits here, EVIL
stamped on his laptop and I don't know
whether it means he's cool or he's evil. He could be.
Complaining about the young is a stupid habit,
it's what really makes you old.
Freckled shoulders, I don't care. I don't take care. I assume
I'll be forgiven. My innate, inchoate value,
which vanished. It's been a long time coming, but in the end it's sudden
(my not being young)—men suddenly
seem aware I won't be the one
to give you sons, and before you know it everything
is walled off but the possibility of violence.
Boy, I get it: I too was raised on those family stories
that explain how although we never did anything we
were brimful of virtue, how it is that in spite of our actions'
wicked outcomes we remain packed with value
like a bank vault full of cash.
I remember what I was never asked to forgive.
How I was made to believe in the good intentions
of our crimes, invested in them, how I must uphold them
against the feeling, worse because more powerful,
of the truth. I still can't stand to hear of atrocity. "If
our American sisters knew," said a voice from Vietnam in 1971,
but we knew, we are able anyway to know,
it just doesn't make a difference. We let conditions
remain conditions because we must find good schools
for our kids and anyway our
suffering could do no one good, we would
suffer for you for nothing! And nothing
could be worth the worthless
sacrifice of a white woman's comfort.

I never know what's at stake, only that I can't risk it.
White men are so scary! This one sitting here next to me
swathed in pristine tech, immaculate sweats. The rage!
My sweetness and light loses his toy, falls asleep on my arm.
I am all the ego and tragedy of comforting.
There's no way to be worth this light you're in.
Step aside and it shines on a surface unseen
in whose reflection you see the bargain of your birth:
gratitude and silence. It is a promise:
you must refuse to suffer for an instant your knowledge.

2

Have faith that people of goodwill continue,
only their goodwill is for your pale skin, your blue eyes,
their goodwill is for you as a mother of white babies
as once it was for you as a white baby girl, a future wife
for one of many sons brought up on guns,
a wife thus a target, and eventually, if you survive,
another woman to step on the necks of young women,
and who can tell by looking that you're not? You're not
theirs, you say, you're not drowning the past
in the trunk of a burnt-out cypress,
you're not a burial in the form of a woman.
Or are you a burial and is that better. Am I a glacier
or could I be a field, mantle of earth
lying calm above the battlefield, a *once*
you visit and forget.
My uncle said a hateful thing. He was playing with my son,
it hovered around him. I made the face
I face it with, an expression I do not wish to keep,
but I've spent half my life making it,
it becomes me. Can I take back what was done (they said) for me—
my undreamed value demanding
toppled gods and a world on fire.
Can I take that value to the bank
and buy a home or a few hours of babysitting,
or an ounce that saves the life of someone else?

3

Mitch McConnell says no one alive
caused slavery or got a penny from it
or bore it or was enslaved—not sure
what form of words you did use, sir, to say
you don't know how the past works, how close it breathes
riding on the next horse over in fact and tugging yours
to the river, its hand on the rein and I won't say bone
for she's very much alive, our past, her smooth skin
pink at the cheekbones, blush roses, she's smiling
so you can't help smiling back; she's a white mother,
so in your book a good thing though you claim
not to know her—"Ah never met that laidee"—ah but you did,
and I did too, and I'm wearing her jewelry
which is how I know someone alive who profited from slavery,
I'm looking at her in the black glass
of the midnight river in midwinter.
I came down here to drown a semblance,
a person like myself who was so pretty,
a person-like piggy bank
with a perfect mouth into which you place a coin.
She'd been instructed to keep her place,
John Wayne will rape you otherwise
well that wasn't quite the threat but you know
something similar, cold and dirty,
too cold to be acknowledged, too dirty to hear,
so when my mother says she loves John Wayne I think she means
she knows better than to disagree with him
when he says something stupid about Indians—
it's very important to agree with John Wayne about the Indians—
now I write this out I can see how stupid it is!
How thin and yet a prison lasting, for this white lass,
nearly forty years. For this white loss. Well what's next?

4

A cross in the road arrests me with a stranger's loss.
Once I shook—not shook, no, but snatched up my son
and he was so startled that I, Mother, would do such a thing
I never will again. Have coffee
with your mom. Don't get mad at her because of how
she votes, she votes vindictively, but don't get mad.
Who should get mad if not me?
A witness could explain what went wrong if there were any.
You did what you could, I know,
make a song of it; you did
the best you could
but it wasn't good enough.
I'm a self, not a stem, not a passage through.
A temporary daughter builds a lifelong stranger,
her heart a soundproof room.
I keep leaving this place and coming back.
Crossarms draped with fake morning glory.

5

So good-bye to the decades of innocence. What
is innocence? Safety, ignorance. Nothing
to be proud of. An innocent can believe
anything. I believed that good took care of itself,
justice, you know, in the weft.
And if there is no justice, will love or harmony
or neat garden rows or good wine or vows of silence
or hardening your heart and choosing your words
or a goldfinch come early on a purple coneflower,
will it come, will it do, will it rescue you?
The goldfinch has an unfamiliar, theatrical cry.
A bumblebee thrums in a box of bloom.
He flies only as well as is necessary to reach
the next moss rose, bumbles in with a shutting off of buzz.
If henbit blooms in a crack am I comforted?
Instead of justice, coincidence—or not coincidence, fullness: that any gap
invites presence, a green that gropes in from elsewhere.
I am trying to make peace with that gap though.
It says nothing as I lob words at it;
it opens wide, chewing on forever. "My wuv"
my son repeats after me; accuses me
of a messy kiss.

THE YEAR IN PICTURES

There was endless suffering for some in those years.
Those who lost everything came to stand at the end of the world,
and their voices echoed back from there, saying
How do you stay
when our messiah has fallen into the void?
We stayed still at the monitors
knowing we could do nothing, and that nothing
we could do grew, our leaders
saw to it that it grew, a bubble separating us
from the rest.
We were wild with grief—but quiet. Cracks in me
through which one thing and another grew. I'm still
pulling out these shoots.

⁊

When bombs fell on Baghdad in 2002
and I suckled myself in my narrow bed and felt
cut off, unwilling, civically dead, and said nothing, then
I was in the habit of crossing Ford Parkway Bridge
to get to work, gazing with no care at lovers and fighters
holding signs about war and trouble when I
was not in war or trouble, or love;
not in love, living on air, pretty, dead, not there,
the summit of a certain white kind of thing,
my hair the rippling red of a nuclear river.
I scorned them, middle-aged do-gooders
holding up signs about Palestine
and making no difference, no difference
in the passing, the traffic, no difference at all to me.

⁊

People board tiny boats, push out into the sea.
Blue deepens below them, how little it takes
to tip in. Once seen, you can't unsee the needless death.
Drowned three-year-old, you know the one.
You don't know the one because now there is another one
and by the time you read this there will be another,
another, another and another.
No end to the awful
imagination of man.
Not the imagination. The action. And the inaction.

౷

The vile people exile their grief at life.
They build a wall between one side of themselves
and another, between the god our father
and that relentless wolf our mother.
They make her pay; they purchase motherlessness
in coins that clang like dumb lead on the counter, purchase it dear
and gift it to all, that state of standing
on your own two feet while the seas rise and rip
away your standing, while heaven falls to pieces
on your head. But your own feet! If anyone would come
between you and the storm that cleans its teeth
with your name, let them be executed with dirty wire,
let them be buried thirty feet deep
in debt, let all mothers suffer their milk to dry up
and stiffen into a fossil fuel, let them feel
how powerless love is before violence, before
a generation who refuses to care.

౷

TRUMP is moved by a picture he has seen
of one kind of a suffering in a suffering world.
TRUMP has not looked: there are many pictures,
many unpictured, ruins buried up a mountain
eroding with a century's rain. I read

of a man who unearthed his mother's teeth.
He was away when his village burned.
They killed everyone in his family. Now
he builds his house where death
came to her children before her; his children play; his mother,
I am his mother and I take comfort
in my surviving son. To have one surviving son
is to know there will be joy again among us,
an us to say our names
as he gathers our teeth from the ground.

๛

They cling to power like a cicada's skin to a concrete stair.
The monster has climbed out the slit and left with
his new damp wing case hanging useless on his back
like a coffin—walking down Pennsylvania
carrying another man's coffin
or a woman's, a big one, big enough for
a mother and daughter, a pair of sisters.
They crawled under the wire
or they came in through the gate.
They claimed to be people though we couldn't tell
with their odd looks and strange speech.
On exam, we discovered they had ovaries,
wide pelvic bones that birthed. A glitter spangling
those bones was a necklace once, or the remains
of a glass pane they fell through, the pain
that fell into them. Unraveled,
this flag's a mere skein of skin.

๛

Today another outrage perpetrated in my name.
I'll get up from my desk and walk
into the street and we'll all be there,
we'll refuse our past and come pouring out
from the custody of office buildings as if a bomb's

gone off—boom! and we come pouring out,
laying down our money, flooding the streets.
Wordless we walk toward the capitol
on streets green with renunciation.

෴

We are reduced to voting, divided by liking. I indicate
with a gesture my choice, a little flag falling on a familiar name,
but I want something else, multifoliate genitalia
fronted on one gorgeous herm-headed
deity to rule with their strange organ, a bevy of breasts
gushing milk into a million mouths. That is my choice!
So I ride my ownership toward a share.
I struggle to loose a sight
not already accounted for and sold back to me.
A sight not banked, a sense organ that's wet. I want
a field, a horse; a fence, his shirt caught and torn on it;
a naked soldier who drops his gun and runs
away to the infinity of his mother's arms.

෴

My big healthy daughter sleeps upstairs
her arms around a stuffed octopus, okay—
she terrifies me. Any army,
we are mere flesh before these men.
I know, they're our men—this year.
The boys from S4 go marauding again.
Give them swords and they'd lay waste
for the fun of it. They don't know, and how are we to tell them
your mother loves you with tenderness
for the tender parts of you, not the hard parts
or she should—and likewise everyone
is treasured in a mom's arm or should be and so
think of her before you strike.
I don't think that makes much difference. I don't know
how you make people see other people.

I mean, men kill their mothers! And some mothers . . .
These boys are five and six, and if I did see
one kicking the other in the street it's not worse
than trying to kill your brother in the backyard,
which I did. If I saw them sleeping
I wouldn't think of soldiers. I'd think of boys.

∽

When the ambulance drives west toward your school,
I'm the bird squalling above it. I'm the feather
falling from the bird, I'm the mite on the feather.
I am the promise that every other future
might be traced from this moment, I'm the feather,
I'm the bird, I'm the school bus that's stuck in a river
and the river threaded through that bus, I'm the mercy
you might have, the wayside stranger, I'm lucky
and I'm the mercy. I'm a nightmare. I'm the North Star
and both poles for any disaster that might befall you. I'm the river.
I swirl over your catastrophe, I make the best of it.
I'm halfway to the sea before you know I left.
I'm never coming back.

∽

I creep up to the scene of someone losing everything.
Sister-mother, I want to say we are connected in radiance,
a thin web compared to the superstructure
in which my interests pluck at yours. Your world
collapsed because that was expedient in mine
or at least not inconvenient, so how can I mourn
your not being close enough for me to care more?
But having read your loss I can't unsee it.
It shot through to the depth of me
a splinter never to be plucked free.
Your daughter! I carry her wherever I go,
whatever that means, whatever it may be—
her memory in me an alignment of atoms,
the turning of an infinitesimal sail.

My baby, let this little world go on forever, if no other has.
Your parents lie in geologic strata
under an inland sea
where you plunge amid strange things that swim
over their sleeps. Oh what do I mean. Time,
but not time, violence, the accumulated leavings,
anger of men or mere anger, our empty cities, Troy or Skara Brae.
They leave nothing. The army sweeps like a broom
and thousands of years on no one speaks the tongue
she blessed her last baby in, kissing her head and saying
as I say to you, I will always love you and my love will be
with you until the end of time. She latches. Flow
blooms. "Fwoom!" as the doctor
says his wife said to him, with fingers of firework.
She leans back and falls full into me.
With my son I read of dinosaurs, the comet, extinction.
I could almost weep for the hadrosaurs,
those defenseless cows.

Messiah

I see my son try to be human and it's so hard.
He's clawing his way up a mountain,
his fingers scraping root, gravel, anything to haul
him another inch into this world.
He's three. I cradle his being,
what the world will make of him. He watches the blade
as I trim his nails. A man on the news
was never loved enough; easy for me to say
as I buff one ragged cut smooth so it won't
catch. His mother loved him, even stands beside him
. . . no, that's his wife. It seems a man sometimes
will be a beast for all the women in his life. We don't
make you better. When you were born,
I understood that old promise: how you hold
a seed of infinite change and I must
do anything to bring you to bloom.
Is that what your mother did, tyrant? Is this your flower?

BRIDE

Mother cowers, afraid
of anyone in a hoodie, and it's all right
for her to be afraid because her fear is one thing she has,
one power her men must nod
their heads to, they nod their heads,
they are watching a woman tortured on TV and she
(washing dishes in the background) expresses her
fear of a man in a hoodie. They nod. The tortured woman
gasps—but I can't do it, I'm sorry, I should try
to make you feel what they don't
watching that scene, that beautiful woman
playacting an apex of suffering at the direction of a man to make
serious viewing for other men that
expresses to them some rightness: right
that men should have women to torture to express
the extremity of their views—remember it's acting—
she gets a prize—and mother in her used-up
voice complains from the doorway—too old
to torture, she's outlived her usefulness as a sacrifice
just as you are outliving your martyr days
and entering the years of dishwashing; her voice
winds in from her cave to the dark theater
where men watch the world breathless, arrayed
in her bridal finery for them.

SAINT

A monk stuck in a cave for seven years
got scurvy, he got crazy. Women brought bread
and lemons and said,
"That poor boy." Then he got light
about *our* sin, sin, sin! I don't want to go on.
It's obvious women are the sewer because we
mend: I've cut apart my old comforter cover
and I'm turning the sheets as in the old days, sewing
two halves of the moon along a new middle, making
a coverlet for my boy so he can learn
how to rest under human comfort. My son
who, goddess help me, will never be
a fucking monk or stockbroker, he'll be
a father, brother, lover, friend, he'll tend a lemon tree
I'll show him how to keep alive through winter
in a sun-filled window. My son, let me show you how to hold
water in your hands to bring it to anyone
(plant, child, woman) who needs a drink
in this comparative desert.

BODY ALBUM

The weekend purls away, my son wants to go to a playground.
"We could go to a playground. That"
(waves hands) "something we could do."
Which tells me how I talk about the possible.
Our little home is a shell I carry on my back.
I scold, I hug. It's September, then March, April, and
inward his sister crafts her fetal rebellion.
I pray for her to come and kill the meanies,
but they thrive. Daughter of my hard year,
she feeds on what runs in my blood.
It's 2017, I'm lousy with revelation.
We buy apples. He cries, I survive. I live
in an acre of litter. I keep a threat in reserve, my coiled *if,*
I keep my hands ready. I fear everything. I don't feel
like a person all the time now. Asking
for help, he's always asking. Help! Whining about colors
I will not help. He's learning nothing, I give him nothing,
The Nothing knocks at the door.
I want to be alone, a horrible wish.
I'm not a horrible person, it's a terrible moment,
intolerable, abominable mom. I'm living better
than whole graveyards. I hold my own hand
to be held or to hold me back, I don't know which. I'm
in the kitchen scraping a crust from a dish. My daughter
rises like yeast inside. She's such life.
But how can she bloom here where I'm lost?

Her Birth

Driving in from a world without you,
we are calling the midwife.
I swim up to the surface of things to tell how I feel
but I can't find my old tongue.
So it's now. In the triage room with a blossom
my left hip comes free.
The nurse has the name we mean to give you, Leigh, so I know
it's true, I'm having you.

Lines I might write between the flows,
I bit the pen and counted.
Decisions I might make awake to my next suffering.
Arrow in me, once lodged so neatly,
now where might I place our undoing
between one gas station and the next on the moonlit highway.
Where might we enter the old order.
Messiah, this night of your birth goes by forever.

To whom does this pain belong? Your wingspan crushes
my womb, my limits burn and turn hard
as stone, I'm pressing my forehead against the false marble wall
waiting for the hospital elevator.
I used to be a person but am become a wave
that breaks; am contraband, a double body, film
of thought wrapped around an action that gains traction,

that spins motion, that makes you.
Fuck, I want to sleep for days now, and I won't sleep
for weeks. My great organ folds down.
I foreclose on your forest.
Shebeast, may you change me,
may you be born inconsolable and true.
My uterus folds up behind you like a party tent,

you cross the ghost meridian trailing stars.
What is welcome when welcoming, when setting free?
Not that you must ever remember, Leigh.
Between you and me your birth's
the least coin, a blank from which
nothing comes back, pure act. This moment

mine alone so that it hardly exists. I am buried in action,
my one action with its flesh repercussion.
Come. You need this time and I am willing.
I am unwilling but you need this time.
There is no point talking of will

here in the room of necessity.
Windows to my left hand, it's nine o'clock at night.
The life flight helicopter lands and
someone rips a machine off the wall

as I'm trying to express your great rage, to be its focal nipple.
Behold, this impulse is truer than most,
made flesh. I give up the ghost. Girl, you
come here from forever, you

crown. "Put your hand down,"
the midwife says, urging me to feel
you cry before you're free of me. With moved limbs you climb

up my body to latch, catching
with your perfect tongue the first rung
of your ladder to later. Our cord

resists, your father cuts you
into the world of integers. I cradle your lantern skull, unshaped

by your passage through me, so quick you descended to be

my daughter.

Mastodon

Remember the mastodon in the state history museum?
Air whistled through her huge inside.
By death's accident she stood, though her daughters
were dust, her lineage dust, her great warmth, her stratagems
to survive, her wintry expertise, her glad scent, gone.
I felt the matriarchy when I nursed you, girl,
felt its shadow rise behind me:
its hackles rose on my spine
and I knew that it was
and is, remains, no less a fact than that set of bones.
A goddess brought to bed of a goddess.
The truth of our power, true ghost of our power.
Wing of a manta, dark unfurling
I row out into further dark.
It lives in these dreams of scale—
a sudden storm on the prairie, anything vast
you watch ascend in that distance.
What fortress, whale, wind. What oceanic wreck. Anything
you can't see the whole of. Anything that holds
you—you can't help it—close in its vast breast.

Nursing Songs

You, born expert.
Your hunger my comfort, companion, my madness.
I will never rest again,
you are hungrier than the world is.
North wind, this unending draw of you.

I'm waiting out the midnights until your sleep begins.
I slide you down the beams of my arms
as if I were the moon and you my reflected light.
Then I throw myself down, throw myself down
the mountains into sleep.

I sit for a decade in my glider, my snowy window rocks.
My left hip grinds down to a fine powder, I can't feel,
it can't matter what's left of me.

I'm flying, nothing matters
except the anchor of your sleep
dragging that anchor in the deep

until it catches.

༄

Endless day/night
wandering time, was and is
instant compressed eternal—makes me
think of polar bears, time
in her den, dark
not like the bright world of floes
a soft life of cubs
exists apart from the hunt
Mother, hold in that
time beyond time
mother of time—
Big Bang, Big Smush

desire & flower, pucker & spout, circle
of gift and giving
Hunter, you must learn
how we loved you
with a love beyond the world
love that is the real world,
how a real world grows
from this circle of mouth and milk
Learn what is real
Daughter, revisit
that room under the ice
where you lived with your mother, your daughter
your daughter, your granddaughters
your sister, your unborn daughters, your grandmother, yourself
your last self, your next self
in one body under ice,
you live there still.

Slightly turned smell of milk rises
from you to me. Your mouth leaks it, you have no idea
it runs out. Milk is forever. I dream it
forth from me, a duration that is land.
My labor of holding you becomes
a forest of you, trunks of trees in the forest,
every tree gains a ring
when I lift you to me again.
Time as liquid, time as a gel that builds, each minute a second
kind of time invested above the first. Or is this
the first time, everywhere replaced by another—
programmed, needful, thin,
time as a knife paring rind?
Not time as a goddess or as a geode grown.
Time as a crystal sap I exude.
I make time. Not I personally, but I as a gradient of the goddess,
a passing weather of her. I, a moment's mother. Through me she
drove her chariot, which was time, over her body,
time, under her shining lash, time.

ʣ

Took & weighed you, filly,
fine they declared you,
my loaner from Juno,
flipping and splashing the dish.

My last baby, bittersweet of you in my arms.
Your desire the size of forever, a field
encompassing all the land on this side of the mountains,
dotted with white flowers, false Queen Anne's lace
each flower carrying its own green spider.
A cabin on the hill in which I am singing

Shenandoah while you rise in my lap like a loaf of bread.
With your marvelous eyes you gaze on me,
storm-blue then sea.
Why was I unprepared to be so loved?
My goddess, my girl,
let me die in your arms.

You rise from me like a flower from the grave.
Let them bring us a field to drape my shoulders,
a forest to keep us warm.
Let them bring me the rivers
plucked up one by one from the landscape.
I would take anything to give it to you.

ʣ

My milk runs out. She reaches my limit!
So let me have another baby, another smaller set of needs
so largely felt that I can feel and be her all
until she becomes. I'll go back to the well, fearless, replete,
anything but free—oh for the closet luxury of choosing
anything I want from the hospital menu
for my first meal after I gave you
everything. You slept while I devoured

sausages and hash browns. My ability again endless,
ocean! A tide that runs from under her feet,
ripping land away, overturning her into
endlessness and sleep. Nothing's happy like a baby.

⌒

When did you leave off nursing your daughter?
I would be nursing her still
if we had not had to go on living.

Let me hold her,
all I want is to nurse my baby forever.
Let the world pass through me and sweeten into her,
a silk handkerchief through the eye of a needle,
the whole sea
through a crow's bone.

My milk thins until it's a story.

The Flood

My aunt died. I haven't told anyone.
I see a woman who looks like me, a blue stain on her lips
like she's been saying hello to the Atlantic for hours.
I should call my mother, she should call me—
it's water under the bridge, so much water under the bridge
that the river rises and floods, the bridge slides apart,
everything's swept away and now you're standing
in a wasteland strewn with rocks.
Nothing seems to matter, so you go wandering,
picking up rocks, putting them down, reading
in script grand as a bank,
"I don't love my mother" or "The Patriarchy."
"Oh, so that's what that is," I say,
and put the rock back down in its spot, sand ringed
around it like the force of sound around an explosion
as every tendril of water drains away.
This desert I wander. Buy a card,
don't buy a card; express, don't express
this feeling—what feeling. What feeling? What to say
to the loss of nothing. I put off knowing
what a dead woman could tell me. In the end,
nothing. Who knows what I feel. The bridge
is hanging half in this tree, half in that one.

Velour nebula—my womb expelled, flayed like a vast, bloody fish.
And if I never again conceive, staunch that receptive willingness,
what magic empire might I still build from my blood?
The foot of the placenta peels,
her scar heals as if I were never a mother.
Forge of messiahs, organ whose other end is in the stars!
I refuse to lock this door. Now that I'm old
I'll take up spells.

My last baby nurses at a dry nipple, she is
so mad! She's calling me but I don't answer because
my mouth is full of mud. I've turned to stone. I've turned
to a name on a stone. I've turned from her to the long after.
If only I could be sure you'd survive me! My friend Danielle
read the highway sign, *This stretch tended in memory*
of such-a-one, and she said "I can't wait for that,"
not so much to be dead but to know it all came out okay,
and okay, yeah, to be dead. I'm impatient to be dead
but still warm, sending back
light from the life I loved so well—
my life on earth, god! To have it done and all
right, to have been
everything for you and to be done trying to be
anything more, to finish, to fade
into a roadside rife with little white daisies,
with asters in the fall and goldenrod dried to a puff.
Fatal call of cardinals—a trail, burble of water,
some trash, bag of bones. Web spangled with dew,
my name weathers away. I fall,
flaw of my flock. I'll be more myth than mother.

Orchard

She has her third ear infection of the season. Her shriek
shatters the house, the house abandons us,
we are sitting on the beach at the end of the world.
My night was an oblivion of fear,
my hip is a shattered globe,
I write out of desperation—
my country sunk in graft, murder, my beautiful friends
scattered, suffering, nothing grows but kudzu.
My daughter was born last year already.
I have so much to put away, to wash, fold, and put away,
to wash, the housekeeping never will be done.
For my birthday I get a book on the Spanish Civil War.
The author takes a measured view—both sides to blame,
"Strange things they did over there in the past,"
as if radical action were entirely a failure of the past
but the radical history is the right one as you well know
so it must be avoided because it leads to action.
My hip calves off along the back of my body,
my night shivers a fever of half-thoughts.
My child is climbing my everything,
climbing the tree of my mind
so I must furiously grow
this apple she's seeking.

GHOST ACRES

Sunlight on the Bogerds' maple turning.

Places recall each other, but then there is no division.

I have lived long enough to know a moment calling out

to a moment though twenty years burn

between entwined atoms. In my lifetime, this house, my house, was built

on a raw parcel my neighbor says he wanted split. What came

before that? An orchard, ghost acres. Like a bulb, my mind had layers, was

a divided place. Does water within water remember its provenance, how it rose

and through what clays and bones?

I had ideas my other ideas didn't know about.

You want to know about the land, why, it's all one place.

You want to know about yourself, where you stand, why?

Because it limits your share? Now it's my maple's turn.

She readies her flamboyant age. We turn our faces up.

"Not Mike—David. David died young. So those were Vern's kids.
Or Ted's kids." She keeps cutting her daughter off, she
needs to get through it for some reason. Famous dead voices entertain us. Oh
a voice is never dead, she said, having seen what I have seen, a voice
can only be lost from not having been heard. "Sweetest woman
I ever met in my life." My kids' books about oceans are optimistic
though the sea has swallowed not only whole families
but everyone except the mother sometimes . . . If it was only the mother
that's a story I could read with both eyes. If a mother can have a daughter and tell her
who was who and whose and have her listen
then I think you can die content. I won't listen to my mother.
Maybe I don't want her to think she can die?
I promise her nothing but upheaval, everything over the seawall.
Well, anyone with a moral idea deserves it.

The Deed

To own this land? How wind passes over it—to own that. Sun,
to own its heat, or how rain considers, addresses, redresses this ground; to own
the shapes wind makes in these trees. And the view of trees,
my neighbors' trees, in winter the trees rising beyond the road there . . . To own
the grasses in their varied gait over the ground, leggy or sidelong, their seed,
the birds which come to feed on that seed, to own seed and trees
and feathers that fall and yes, each flight path
over my land, dove's down-cropping swoop from my pecan tree . . .
Deeply, too, to go and own the water that flows below—no,
I don't own the water. But bones, I own those:
tender outline of baby rabbit laid down and earthed in. And I own the roots,
deep tap of pine, twine of maple, and the fungal web between.
You too, now: I own your long glance as it follows the blue flash of that bird that's briefly
mine. Light of the moon, that too, her lumen laid over flagstones in my front yard.

Meridian

Shall I break my well-tended silence now and for what reason.
To mend, and in mending incidentally to lie, or to lie low?
A titmouse bathes in slant light, quotidian, quieted
amid the shaking vocation of late leaves . . .
But if a bird categorically described as gray can be seen to convey
the faintest whisper of iridescent blue, who then might you yet be?
Becalmed, will I miss the moment of passing.
But how could I miss it if it was meant for me.
I'm almost ready for nothing,
to honor her plans that are not mine, I mean my life's.
Learn from birds who drop
from spanned to folded, pristine, that viridian head, dead in an instant.
You too, your heart was built in a clasp, came to in a spasm already
pulsing through the infant medium of you.

Fidelity

The field gives way to the forest gives way to the fire, or the eye.
I'm traveling an edge. It's close
and yet to feel the ragged limit is difficult; to stop to know it,
impossible. Impossible leaf-edge of infinite detail
placed against the myriad members of my skin
so I ken its ownings innerly but no image
archives in my lossy mind; I am lost
in learning what is immediately forgotten, what cannot at any cost be kept.
(Depths marked, one goes almost immediately in above one's head)
(We were supposed to push up silt with our feet
when we waded out from shore for fear of
stingrays. It was hard to remember—not
hard to remember to be afraid but hard to remember
to act on that fear)

I saw air strikes fuzzy, gray, on the classroom TV in 1990. It was someone's life
I was watching pass. It was felt to be necessary, this demonstration
in heat-seeking pixelation. Looked like a video game, but it was Social Studies.
Other times, we learned about Mesopotamia, where it all,
whatever it was, began. Our parents drove everywhere. I can't find
anyone's hand in the dark. Nothing waves back from the lake
when you finally find it again, and it's so shallow, is it even the same water. I have so many
memories that don't make sense. This morning
while I lay in bed I did a quiz called Would You Survive a Bear Attack? and
it said I did fine but I can't help noticing I got the pivotal questions wrong, like whether to stand
and yell or run or what. I just won't hike in the back country, then. I won't go.
I'm here for three more lines demonstrating a sensibility like we built them
in the last years of the twentieth century and broke them down
in the first years of the twenty-first. No one knows what they'll do until they do.

We looked at our cell phones to find the route laid for us by police for the protest.

Whatever they said, we could still love each other, couldn't we?

I was busy raising children, my own children

but they were all my children, only some I didn't know yet.

Some couldn't love me back which is the essence of children.

But sister, I was kept busy by the devil in me.

If it didn't belong to me I couldn't love it, said the devil,

if I couldn't control it I would suffer. My heart vibrated in red pixels, it cried those plinky tears.

Wherever we went they were with us, a troop of cartoon devils,

my mother sent some more in a box when I strangled mine.

"He's your son too!" cried the mother of the young Black boy

who had a gun waved in his face, giving us all what no one could hold and the arms

I would in any other world have extended toward him and her

remained at my side and I tried to mother him from a safe distance.

I was led to believe in the beautiful.

My anger has a translucence that exhausts me.

Hateful people have taken over,

their dreams are shit and we live in their dreams.

Lovely, my child: a wrinkle, a stir, a body in a stream.

My hand mirror shows a tangle of ashen roots.

We are all moving the world out, or does it say mourning.

There is a Lightsey of decay who wrote these words

and a Lightsey of repair coming back to make them out.

I don't write enough. But I'm here now, aren't I.

My son asks why he can see the moon in the day.

So now I'm holding an orange and turning it in my mind

projecting a laser onto it from my third eye—some part of me moon,

some part sun, some part the earth I'm flying on.

That's a golf course though you'd take it for a Civil War battlefield,

so green and rolling. Grackles broker a texture against winter's unfamiliar

flash of the ridgeline, inner dark and outer dark

and the thin skirts of trees

and knowing yourself for a flicker

and knowing yourself for a thing in time.

Then I had an interest, finally, had grounds.

Then my lawlessness was sold to the law—one more loss in a field of loss.

An hour between wars, my daughter falls heavy on my chest, but was there ever an hour

between wars?

My mother runs away through the underbrush . . .

I take a break for lunch, let her get a head start,

hear her crashing, then silence, then crash.

Houseless, a wren tucks under our eaves. My children peer, their laughter restless lightning.

Joseph goes to bed. Abandoned! Being alone—it means *I'm* here.

A person trying to appear, I swear, but rarely by.

What was I told that could guide me now? Keep the silverware, if it's silver,

in a green velvet bag, I've got the bag, I've got a whole world that eats

from my hand, I'm half granary though I'm going bare—

it haunts me I can't replace them now, my children.

I should have another just in case, have one this last year.

As if one more wouldn't be a case too! I'll always be desperate,

with this collapse zone that passes for a heart—and send a salvage mission for the rest of it,

my "self"—self, what was it? a set of pretty habits, a list of wants, a little landlocked

princessipality. A woman in her forties can't do anything right, there's nothing right

to do. I've gone for one run and drunk three bottles this week. I almost lost Jack, his

running shape winked from view. Would I were a root, could split. What was whale

spins as she sinks, drifts, nicked by nippish teeth as she descends to this abyssal plain.

Humility

My mother in her forties, she didn't belong to the world.
She didn't say a word to me about that colossal gap.
Once she bled on an airplane and asked me, as she went
before me down the aisle, if it showed. It didn't. Mom,
I didn't know!, you were suffering
I'm still trying to know. Even when I'm past done I'm still trying . . .
She was wearing white pants, which when I remember,
white pants on an airplane, you must still have had hopes.
You were what, forty-eight? Which seems young, or at least
close enough for compassion.
Do I, now the mother, belong more to the world than you did?
I belong nowhere because I was placed nowhere.
Everything, room and time for everything can be found still.
It all narrows down to one bleed.

Endurance

It was not an immoral way to weed a patch.

How to raise a child, I understand in principle, I could describe it.

To have a house is not immoral either, only lucky.

Yet every day I'm revealed to myself as if I had become a corporation,

so endless and entwined a subsidiary in that country pollutes the ground

while this one designs a policy to exclude Black women from good maternal care.

But I cannot be pulled back: in infinite fields my tendrils climb, in every river

my herbicidal capillaries seep, and every day I can lie down

in the knowledge of another failure, another place the poisons leaked through me.

What, should I be a dam?

Of course I should, of course.

The children deserve everything, the world, whatever else I serve, am yoked to.

Anything I can stop I should.

Anything I can do I should.

The work is still to be a soul who has at least seen herself from a distance.
With water and wind our house quarrels, banks its forty years' holdfast.
To be a mother and at the pit of the mother nothing but smoke in coils.
Jack reads in pavement the cracks and freezes of distant weather
and I remember when any flaw

any exception, leaf skeleton or quick dog's bolt across setting
stone was a sign of life, that something moved beyond what we knew
(cans of food keyed by hand then one day scanned at the A&P).
Am I outside your knowledge or am I its bounds, the sky into which you fall.
Am I the woods or the frost that stalks through them?

I'm the insect dead on the screen, any minute tragedy;
tulip tree dropping yellow leaves over school grounds sodden and cool,
am evidence of weather, ice that etches, a scrim of voice
that comes back from the well saying "She loved you and she always will."

Last night I heard someone laugh with a silvery splinter of icicles

like a woman who'd given up on everything.

Probably it was an owl, it went on until I fell back asleep.

I never felt December so deeply. I record no dream as I have had none.

"Oh no, oh no!" my daughter cries when she wakes. Well, she dreams.

I'm feeding eight pigeons this morning, my ground's alive with their bobbing.

Everyone's concerned about the future, but the past isn't over either,

it veers, it shakes, we wake up crying "Oh no, oh no!"

The ground full of its _____

To arrive at a shore knowing _____

Embroider the letter until it slips.

And the true kept being true (this endless

mostly private journey toward a voice) (and once I had come to it, would my

arrival set you, a real you, free?)

So hard to tell whether it could be a poem I could write.

It's October, now December, and soon just winter—

a tree and candles for a little while, then

the long dark. What will I give, I don't know yet.

Stop COVID in prison, said the sign, then they sold the house and someone

took the sign down. What I know to be true, or rather what I

understand. Me now, I wanted almost to touch that blank of despair so I would know

the worst. As if you still *know*. As if the machine works underwater.

Then my son woke crying to think one of us might die

and I could say only, "You're right to be afraid."

I'll never forget it, I'll never remember, I didn't see this coming, so I keep listening.

My life as it was is gone. Myself. And you, yours. Overcast dawn: notice again

how pines sigh in wind. Ice in birdbaths shatters, my

children cracking that skin. Highway, mists out there, people go by too fast.

Paradise

Silent under the Christmas tree my daughter gazes up into angels.
We are warm here, we just turn up the heat if not. She's quiet
because she's thinking, which is new to her—not repose
but inner lightning. Then something descends, all-eating, all-obscuring.
What are we raising them for? For the machine to eat,
to be rich and cruel, to be good workers? Then why
raise them at all? My husband turns up the heat in passing.
You can't choose. Speckled birds flit around the thistle feeder,
countless, poor, hungry, rich, replete, assured of death.
What meadow will come when seeds fall, I plead for.
She runs off, a wish, a flash. What mends. What aches? What long-ago wrong
I did, wound I took. I can change my life,
I can certainly change my garden. What answers me.
Build a forest branch by branch. This will outlive me.

"The lap" she calls it as if this artifact of how I'm sitting lives apart from me.
My daughter loose in the morning house, which smells
why I don't know like my grandmother's house now—
her thumb in her mouth as she re-finds her objects, renews her language.
Yes, the lap lives apart from me as her life is apart from mine,
as I become salvageable for her, not a person but a trove. My fledgling,
goddess bless her scavenging! May what shines stay true
a rock from a stream that never dulls.
(A loud boom of thunder last night woke me
but how, I asked Joseph, did I know what it was if it woke me—
seems you'd be just awake by the close of the sound, knowing nothing.
Maybe, he said, you hear all the sounds when you sleep,
your mind filing them immediately to be forgotten—
imagine a life passing that way, as a storm in the night)

Wreath

Sometimes I'm stunned, as when a little bird settles on the windowsill
here—reliably buff underbelly of the chickadee, as if no
time has passed since I first saw him. I
am always trying to appear, but my appearance flowers from some source
unknown. News of last week's shooting fades amid crumbs—I shuffle and stack that old news,
a remnant sprayed gold by my grandmother. Would anyone stop me folding up
into the dried cone wired to the tree that never bore
such a gold pome? Inner distances I'm after, outer distance into which
I'm sunk. I live as I am able. Now the season is past, the Christmas tree is down; time
to put away ribbons and gold paper. I will keep an eye on the far field.
My girl needs the pieces put back together, she's contrite.
What's broken can be mended, the music reminds us
and if broken for good, remembered,
and if forgotten, then forgotten.

Winter Solstice

I dreamed I was going to deliver a baby I didn't remember growing.

Since you ask, my caution comes of my unnatural dominion.

I'm listening to a field whose language I keep forgetting I'm undoing.

A person speaks in the language of her time the thoughts of her time,

never mind this is a terrifying time. Don't talk to me about revolution, I have children.

My son cried at 4 a.m., I don't know why. "Why are you . . . Did you just . . ." I crawl

in with him for half an hour. I was a dreamer, thus I was a skeptic, thus I was a believer, I carried

my dream by the arm back to my room, took a long drink of it,

couldn't find it in the morning. There were 3,426 deaths yesterday.

But who hasn't dreamed and then woken, who hasn't lived in a spell to see it broken?

If with one hand trailing in the water, if this hand

can become a fin, if a gesture can swim, and this road become a river,

I would understand where it comes from, I would get to the bottom of it.

All week I've been rising to a star which turns out to be a planet.

I dream of my life which wanders away, a wild horse in a field

and I'm holding her bridle—impossibly tall she turns her head

so I can see every arcing lash and I'm left

with the golden loop in my hand. Bend my own neck? I dreamed I was going to deliver a baby

only I couldn't feel you in me. People were talking and I needed to listen

to you but I couldn't find the thread of the soon-to-be, I dream

of my life which is a spell still, I dream of my life.

Between eyes and leaves a blossom took hold. She fell from her bed last night, cried, crawled back in. Drink a glass of water, trace a delta of drips and runnels with one hand. Where did my water come from? I was going to know. I live on the surface of things, ignorant, essentially secure. Birds flew into the window because they saw branches inside. Now silent, one sparrow. "That bird is dead." Yes to the rudimentary sentence we learn from the book. I survive. Little jolt of sunlight cuts one day of January apart from the others. I've never been so meaningless. Follow the path of the cut to higher and lower. Night shrivels to last shadows under bushes. How will I amend the shadows that build behind my children? 3,600 dead in a day. Normal, now, to have lost one in a thousand. Not my one, but yes, my thousand. I know, but I don't understand. How to hold her would make your hand lighter. What limit will I cross in an instant to come through to the other side of breath when someone lifts my body into fire. I have faith in the future even so.

A figure in a yellow coat appears on the frosted lawn.

Something in the dream that didn't hold your weight.
Rain down to an occasional handful. We rise tired. I can't
think in shapes anymore so I come here to the page.
I'm trying to learn which chances to take. "To ride out
in any weather" —that line rings in my mind, why.
I was sent a dream to get through it, but the pieces don't keep.
I lived on a distortion that came true, a fault line.
Are you waiting for something more lifelike to be called your life?
Yesterday I learned there are faults and yet deeper faults
that undermine them. I am
deeply undermined, a prioress
immured in a cell that becomes a cliff.
Your life having gone by
now you see, from your barred window, a sea in which you might drown.

Last night I had to snuggle her back to sleep. When? Maybe 2 or 4.

Now 10 a.m., a meeting, a fresh marketplace for these needs and capacities.

The *city* of capacity, a place where you and I might go for a drink, Suzanne—

who the fuck cares who I used to be, am I right? A leaf on the wind.

I want a pedicure, a manicure, you know, touch.

I want tolerance. But did it ever exist? Did anything? Good question.

How was your weekend? My weekend? You mean it's over?

Life had a lot of momentum back then, you kept going, you just had to.

Now I'm free to cuddle my strange beast. What kind of free? She's getting stranger.

Keeps saying she needs more people. I miss them too, strangers. Me, I have a lot of range,

I mean rage. I'm so afraid for them, my son, I'm afraid the world wants them

asleep, dazed, grazing in a fed hunger. I'm so mad when he disobeys. I want him to see it

my way. Not a poem! If it were a poem, I'd be in it,

being a good mother.

Valentine's

In the right light can I be for a moment who I was when I first knew you—
that girl betrayed me more than one way but I still love that boy.
I help our children with paper and paint—they are
you and me, a thread that extends through us, past us.
Twin moons to our pandemic planet, we revolve, missing
each other at every turn. This is love but also now something else, kinship;
you are my second self, "husband" the word for the one who appears
in the doorway when a child cries. Sometimes the first, sometimes the second
person to rise and attend to them. Sometimes *I*, sometimes *you*.
Still you seem to have an unchanging tilt of the head toward me
as if I were the star you'd trained your observation on.
If two lines seemingly parallel continue to meet—
if we are still lovers and can arrive on that stage
to improvise with each other for the audience of each other
If I am still your choice and I could choose none other

Honesty

Gave up on what was in the dream to find.
A shadow of the mind, an inkling too dim to keep.
If I put true with true will the whole ring?
No, because in the relation lies arise. My mother's sister
died so fast she must have been surprised.
Light needles between ranks of pines,
mine and my neighbor's, my other neighbor's—
they're building a house between us and it troubles me.
Why? I don't like perfect things.
I don't like the present pretending to own a better past.
Every join I try has a crack in it.
Fugitive, I'm in recovery from some wound
I gave myself. You know what they say: the deepest
ravines begin at home. But who else can I trust to touch you?

Being a white middle-class mother has not made me good—shh, I think it's a secret—or at least

unsayable if obvious to people not in the magic circle drawn every ten minutes by a

white middle-class mother—yes I feel that interrupted—draw it again—again—in a

life where difficulties arise it is hard to be good! and increasingly I don't know

where good lies—cresting far out to sea, whooing

from the woods, wavering in midair like the pole star that

moves—fuck you, Ursa Minor!

Sanitized my perceptions are so dull—unsanitized they're lethal

and am I, I, this set of biting deviations from the corporate incorporeal mother

I am seemingly unable not to become—her disciple

in every kitchen, bedroom—fucking the succulents—but I still

love myself in spite of all that tells me not to

love myself not in approved fonts or sayings to hang on kitchen walls

love though not blazoned or a flag over my house, flag over my house, flag over my house!

Shots late last night, someone on the LISTSERV

pinpoints them at Sovereign, somehow worse to know

where. Stars in their density buzz. Our watchword carries an old slur. Exchanging it, you enter

the devil's house, his shifting walls charged with the antidote to your bloodstream's rebel flow.

I don't feel safe when you say that. Nothing's safe for long, mom. Keep

an eye on the distance, which once in a thousand years

bursts into flames. I can't keep out of the current.

What's erotic is what's deeply undercut. I say it because I'm lost

and what stirs me is my loss and I try to arrive where it's still splintering

houses, roads into the sea, where something might be saved or at last kissed and sent off.

Supposed to rain on and off for a hundred years and it does, and I rain too.

A person can go on if they do. That's how you know.

A person can't change what a person won't change.

In the curve of the wave something gleams. We grieve ourselves.

I hope my exhaustion can be a poem. Hope is too strong a word.

Jack's Zoom lesson says, "The shape with two long sides . . . " we crawl into it

unspelling one's wishlist / we have blankets / they are also rectangles, baby!

Witness E.'s fear of being a person who makes mistakes;

dear E., is there any other kind of person?

turned broken bent; shed her skin because it didn't take . . . was a lovely one . . . "this yours?" "oh me?"

—iridescent, with big eyes— "no no; you take it"

Once my mother said to me,

"I've been thirsty for years and I didn't know it"

but mostly she didn't tell me anything—fifteen, I wandered through her house like a little storm cloud

and she didn't tell me about the alien core of her, that being who bore me

nine months like it was one hour in which I held my breath.

What must be healed for it to become a poem

Nothing?

Am I the stealthy thief of my life still, reef and lighthouse both.

Resorting to the same words, carrying an old book, reading out lines I marked years ago to tell you

I love you.

Feeling of pregnancy forever forgone, a new organ builds offshore.

What weather thunders in. Midnight shrivels to an offshoot

under the mockingbird's claw. Usual sessions of question and answer

and the gloss is a tangle of briar

at the edge of the common wood. A voice calls a name. It isn't mine but I'll go,

calling us home to the abandoned house. Statue's open hands, outstanding debt. I am

the ruby that slipped into the shallows. Vanish. Listen

for the new birdsong that is not quite the old. Sketch this eclipse.

What was this life I birthed

was brought to me to nurse

grew legs and walked off

New Political Parties

Vote for your gut bacteria. Represent your antibodies before Congress. Ambassadress of ocean, assign yourself an undersea peak that never breaks the sun. Vote for cataracts lanced with sunset that set you back on your human heels— you photographed their shimmering appearances, now vote for them. Vote with the massive intelligence of the aspen, their intimate hand not distant from their distributed mind; vote for the fungi's invisible net of needs met. Represent the park where you learned to swing or the leaves that made the world what it was—burning!—every September of your childhood. Vote on behalf of the cloud that dissolves over your head, its carried-out duty of dispersion, vote for the interests of the drops of separate but no longer separable waters that came from far to your forehead. Represent the provenance of your shoe leather. Vote for the finch at the feeder—you called her here, now vote for her. Vote for the poison ivy whose hands mark no ballot; for the flowers gone to seed in the lawn and their seed, risen and rising again in the hope of a meadow. Vote for the meadow and its future as a forest. Vote for the midnight forest your children wander now.

To rise in the fullness and desolation of the true.

Rain pours, brimming these heavy clays, a ground I can't,

even with the new shovel, pierce. The field of what one can narrows.

The world will never invite you, you will never be forgiven. I can't rehearse that history

of how the gap opened between those who saw and believed

and those who believed in something else and saw something else.

The eternal out there has me now—a lesson, a grasp

clean as the Cooper's hawk I saw pluck a sparrow

like she was lifting a leaf from my lawn. Self

is null, an encounter with claws. Leigh saw it with me. Here she is now, this child—

something bright about her from the making of her lingers,

sticks to her like water to glass, a meniscus, a band of the before, halo

of hereafter. I don't mind working, I mind that I can't live,

that the world isn't whole, that everything is a choice.

shh, I can't talk from this place of roots and laundry

I'm in among the phonemes

handing up bits of shell and bywords, hooks and clothespins and whatnot

sometimes I become enraged

with your not listening or not caring!   enough!   for me!   !

and I picture a future of disaster

unraveling on this jagged nerve field—what fancy words can I claw up to show you how it *wiggles*—

I'm at the mercy of preverbal emotions

like no one who presumes to talk should be, no one who presumes to talk should be

a mother—I'm suffering a nameless electrical

storm of being a used-up bit, a snatch of song

I thought could make you whole.

That mouse nest I poked until she poked back

saying "Fellow mother, leave me the fuck alone!"

Lava Cameo

I hand a sprig of salvia to the woman next to me. Under her shawl
gray strands show, she's someone's mother. I hand her
a sprig of lavender, this disassembled spring we graze like late bees. Not my
mother, she will be mine now: volcano and I throw my
body over hers. "Mother and adult daughter" labels will guess at us and true, no question
will arise between us as I hold and she holds her and me the half-
second more we last, for a being who has begun
to hold others cannot leave off even as the mountain picks herself up to persuade us all to ash.
I wish I had two lives, one to go back and one to go on,
instead of one life that tugs in both directions, one life to live and another in which I have
already died a good death. I crouch alone in this opening to the rest of time.
Cut off its rickety stem yet it peoples out white rootlets in the wet medium of my heart.
Inside it even blooms and I send my tiny daughters
to buzz round this bud of an unborn present.

Nest

The sweetness of being needed and being able to fill that need.

Now is the season that everywhere birds look they see

material; grooming the grasses they are a many-beaked rake.

A nest is a knot time catches on.

How can I give my children parents from another century?

A mother from the future. Like I was weather,

rising and giving my seat to another?

The freedom of the world overcome by the dread of the world. Always the world.

Something gathers in the in-between—a long storm of bird chatter.

Myself as a little piece of things, myself

as a fern growing to a pattern forged by the fall of light in an ancient forest,

myself as a museum curated by myself! at another time for other purposes.

I am human so I am part of the disaster,

am animal so I am part of the future.

Svalbard

Light falls heavy as a full-grown fruit, dull gold, substantial.
I'm all old gold now, my quandaries and beliefs moot in this weather.
Hawklike, my daughter knows me deeper. Fearlessly she shows me
these absolutes we live in: my love, her needs. As if on an arctic journey under a dim star
I'm clutching a rattle box of seeds. Morning's wheel will take me
where I can't go. I follow her tumbling on my robe. I've lived
how I could, not how I couldn't. Now how can I, dim alphabet, spell you?
It's hard to have freedom within weather. Belief in anything is loss at last. Sweet girl,
I do not believe the soul survives. The whole survives as the arrow
flies. You shine like mother-of-pearl. Never more than a single dream
from night's store. Rain finds its way through altered land, my land
finds its way through altered us as we find our way through
the midnight house. There's no forecast for me but to follow you.
I'm lost, a root curled round diamond, groundless. What freedom.

Justice

COVID cases in India undercounted, deaths feared 1M+.

My daughter cries at the least rejection as if she had nothing.

Days later, the crumpled petals of my birthday poppies keep an opalescent sheen.

My aloe is a hand of limp fingers, circumstance

devours my attempts at mastery. A crater fever seared in my son's eye

fills with his tears, my good intentions.

The prosecution "humanized" George Floyd, odd thing to say

though you know what they mean. My house echoes my mother's house

in ways I don't understand, my understanding intermits, surrounded

by lakes of reaction. We were so cautious. ("And what will it take? What will

it take?") Leigh stands behind me now waiting for me to attend her,

I am attending to this little plot in hopes of a process of truth breaking.

Seems it's never equinox, we all fall down, keep falling.

No fact is innocent. A man jogs down our street.

Personhood is a meandering property.

One outlines one's palm with a red crayon. One is five.

The deer stopped in my yard and clipped

new leaves from the phlox; I see his print,

two lobes and a line rising between, clear as a letter.

At every stoplight now a man with a sign. The golf course is full

at 2 on Wednesday, the driving range by 3 on Thursday.

What was it, that standing still long enough to leave a print?

We have quit reporting our symptoms, are

vaccinated, funny word; I've had my shots so I can go back to life

as if nothing ever happened to me so what happened to me then?

Can a question be a lie.

What have I done?

Good for you to be untrue so that you keep reaching.

Easter

This water can be described: a thrust meets a rock. The rock
turns aside water's force for now, sends it off either side and back up over its own
body rushing to meet the rock, making a glassy bulge of water, a bustle almost still;
here cleanly singing forth, here froth, here hard waves marcelled;
a handful of diamonds tossed, snakeskin, a sheeny back being
wriggled out of by some fantastic monster. I just had to yell at my daughter
for hanging from a drawer. I want to be the better mother but I keep getting yanked
into the lower. I want to matter. I have to make them cry sometimes. I'm
looking for understanding. I'm trying not to be scary, I hope
I'm not damaging them, of course I am, I am. I can't write from
here. I can't write from this place where I'm
unraveling on all sides. Where I am subject to another's becoming. I
am not at peak, authorial. Basis, background, making, plinth, substrate,
I bend, my depths pulled down in a pluck from the Grenville basement rocks.

Everything comes to everyone eventually. Not true. Hard to forge
any declarative that yields

truth. What is. Something? Nothing
is. I made cinnamon toast for my daughter. Origin
could be a question if we were explorers. I'm just hunkering. Managing. Humanity
is all over me this year. I am very human. I have to expect less. Control
less. Don't adjust the vertical—that's as true
as this image gets. Calls of birds and so on sketch
pilgrimage to an answer. A face
lifts out there, made of mist and mint. A god, and he's gone. It is never
too late for some things. It is already over for others. Mom,
is this forgiveness, an argument that never ends? I am
tending what comes up. Winding those tendrils with which it climbs.
Climbs whose shoulder, through what fence, toward whose undoing.

Morning's dark: a person who leaves, ribbon in their hair
and the whole green unfolds. Alchemy's entreaty
as if I could deny this world.
Slow collapse hollows the half of a mountain
to make a shell where you (reborn) might arrive—
this appetite of forever for us
always yawning.
Has it happened?
Yesterday the maple released its infants by the thousands.
(Rebecca, I'm weeding your garden.)
They fill my sky with flickering blue
velvet that becomes the cold depth of space
where revolves a desolation of gas giants huge and terrifying.
As if I could deny this world!

Walpurgisnacht

Curls rise in the damp, shot through with silver—
call it silver though it's more the gray
repose of a nameless lake where just now a paddle stirs ripples
as we near a great heron, knowing we will never get closer.
A thought ravages a face in passing. I have someone dying—it's my aunt Mary Etta.
Two words, then three, then a rush like a period,
my twelfth-to-last, as she descends the dark stair, reaches
the last rung on the ladder. Let her go into the store of potential persons, become
a baby I won't have. How old will I get and being that old, what will I have seen,
and what will I never have outgrown, and what will I bear
all that long time? World, rain down
on an old woman crossing a parking lot
who may have forty more years to be
an old woman crossing a parking lot.

Devotion

She was telling me about her fertility journey, as another friend calls it,

& how there comes a time in a woman's life when (I hate this beginning)

her egg supply drops off dramatically, and she said, "And that has happened"

in a clear voice—it was so hard to hear and how could it be, anyway,

that this magic power we mostly did nothing but hold

could shrivel and turn to dust, fail us,

without ever having been invoked—for her, at all, for me, twice only—

if I had an ability and with it I made a family, well that was gone now.

Now I have been trying to learn how to touch

without harm or question or return

could I hold the turning of your life in my fingertips

through any stroke shifting the nerve from thrust to pulse, let it happen

that you supply yourself from the spiral of this contact, beginning

ever over again to mother from the other side.

My son lost a tooth. I was so surprised I didn't know how to be. Was not prepared for the gap it left. And he so calm, held out that little white claw, "It's my first tooth." Blood on the root. I don't know about this life. It's good but what is friendship. What is love. What is light, what dark. Our darkness isn't planetary dark, it's inner dark, technological dark. Our fear is modern fear. How to spin continuance here? It's raining, supposed to rain all day, so here we are at the beginning of something that will extend its magic thread, this day all one unbroken streaming down. Learn from it? Little birds do, they endure. This indoors of ours, does it hold what it should? Is it lifelike? Is it warm? Should I be a fairy? I asked him questions until he made it clear he wanted something eerie to happen, something from the other side. So okay, now I am the other side.

Notes

Infernal Selves

The questions "How could my mother treat me this way?" and "How could a mother treat another mother that way?" are very different in scale, but ultimately they have the same root. As a poet, I'm drawn to the smaller scale, the personal question. There's danger in personalizing world-historical forces—solipsism, psychodrama, a narrowing of the moral sphere down to what is before us—yet I think there's a greater danger that we will fail to see the connections, will fail to understand what we are part of and how and when we participate in these larger currents.

One line that didn't make it into this poem may help frame its drive(s): "What does slavery have to do with the work of American mothers? Everything." I had the thought that the painful tendencies of white mothering in America—coldness, the inculcation of reserve, placing the need to maintain appearance above intimacy, sudden bursts of cruelty—have everything to do with how white women participated in slavery and white supremacy broadly, including the genocide of Native Americans.

I feel I should say, about my ancestors, that they were mostly ordinary people. I say this not to protect my ancestors or myself, not even to compare, but to unsettle: the awful mixes with the ordinary. I'm an heiress in the sense that I have history.

Why Rebecca? I was looking for a place to begin, a place to be from. It mattered that Rebecca lived where I did, that her life left so little mark on official records. I wanted to read defiance into that absence. But for all that I wanted her to be my beginning, I found I couldn't trust her. Edith, my grandmother, Rebecca's great-great-granddaughter, I knew well. I can answer for her as a "good enough" ancestor, let's say; I can carry her, and I do. That's the mending I reach for.

Education of an Heiress

"If our American sisters knew": I have been unable to find the original of this quotation. I thought it was Susan Sontag's "Trip to Hanoi," but no; still, I have the feeling the context was similar.

The Year in Pictures

Always that dangerous blur between writing about inaction and justifying that inaction. Always the danger that in depicting something seen I will be reinstating its status as spectacle. Always the struggle over witness, its purpose, its ethics. But if we never write about the emotional-intellectual landscape we are constantly made to traverse by news, how is that truthful to this time? I have taken a risk here. I have tried to put my witnessing self at the center of the risk.

"Unraveled, / this flag's a mere skein of skin" refers to the art of Sonya Clark, which I saw at the Nasher Museum of Art at Duke University. The flag I saw in the process of unraveling was a Confederate flag, which I transposed in memory with an American flag. I saw the flag hanging on the wall; Clark also creates performances in which she unravels flags with visitors. In an interview with Wendy Hower, Clark said that her art is about "Just slowing down, to think about what has happened here. It took years for us to make the Confederate flag. It's not going to be an easy thing for us to undo." She went on: "I think there's poetry in what we're trying to do together. So the right word matters—which is not to rip, but to unravel. There's a little bit of . . . well, we're picking cotton together" (Sonya Clark, *Unraveling*, 2015, Nasher Museum of Art).

Body Album
"Her Birth": Amanda Nadelberg once read a poem she told us was an anthem. That stuck with me. Births are different, one from the next, as are children. The birth of my daughter was a triumphant experience I had not seen written before. Here is my anthem.

Stefania Heim's *Hour Book* is up behind "Nursing Songs."

"Velour nebula" is for Sarah Fox.

"Orchard": *Re* history, I want to point toward Kristin Ross's works on the Paris Commune and May '68, in which she powerfully demonstrates the need to keep contesting the supposed meanings of historical events. Defeat is not the end of the story.

The woman in the photo is another Rebecca, Rebecca Shoup Darst (1839–1913). She was one of my third great-grandmothers, a generation younger than Rebecca Duncan, and she lived a much different life: Ohio, not Florida; affluence, not poverty; one husband, not two or three. My photo was taken by Martha Hoelzer.

Ghost Acres
"A figure in a yellow coat": This, of course, is Amanda Gorman. I was impressed by the moral clarity of her presence at the 2021 inauguration, or, to use a differ-

ent word, her courage—though it didn't then occur to me how much courage she needed to stand where violence had so recently ruled. (See her article "Why I Almost Didn't Read My Poem at the Inauguration," *The New York Times,* Jan. 20, 2022.)

Cheryl Robinson said, "What will it take?" Thank you, Cheryl, for the push.

"Lava Cameo" shares its name with an Eavan Boland poem. The poems are not siblings, though like Boland I wanted to ask how we might re-enter the past. I was thinking of and reading Boland a lot while finishing this book. Her willingness to write poems that weren't pretty, her priority on pursuing truth, trusting that art will arrive on its own—these were stars in the dark to me. Her death in April 2020 continues to grieve me.

Some poems in *Ghost Acres* are titled for virtues (devotion, fidelity, etc.). This was part of an overall thought about recasting the lives we find ourselves living, about a kind of revolution that begins from here.

Acknowledgments

A poem does not get written without many hands. Over the seven years in which I worked on these poems, many people helped make my life and work possible. I couldn't write if someone else weren't, for that moment, looking after my children; couldn't write if the labor of raising children weren't profoundly shared; couldn't write if I didn't daily talk with people who make me think and feel; couldn't write if I didn't have time, with other people doing other work so I can attend to this; couldn't write if I didn't feel connected to a world my writing can touch. The many midwives of this book include people who held open a space around the work, people who stepped into that space with me, and people who challenged me to widen that space. Friends, colleagues, my children's many teachers and carers, my own teachers and carers, relatives, neighbors, many more people than I can list contributed.

If the above suggests the everyday, the immediate, the mundane, let me also honor the far-flung and the magical. Someone drops a seed, and years later it sprouts and blooms. This thrift, this luck, this leaping connection, seems in some way I can't define to lie at the heart of both love and art. So let me tell a few stories of the many strands that came together in this book.

It was at a reading sponsored by the now-defunct Mothership organization that I first read poems from this book and felt from the response that yes, these were poems, so thank you to Megan Bowser and Julia Green, who organized that event; to my fellow readers; and to the audience.

Jameela F. Dallis once said that she was careful about her ancestors, because she knew they didn't all wish her well, and I turned that idea over, thinking about what it might mean for me, until it became a critical element of "Infernal Selves." Thank you, Jameela.

Maybe twenty years ago, I was fortunate enough to meet Cecilia Vicuña through the good offices of Maria Damon. More gently than I can paraphrase, she told me that I was treasuring a girlishness in my poetic persona, and she wondered if I would let that go. I think I finally have understood what she meant, and so thank you, Cecilia.

M. C. Hyland and I met years ago in Minneapolis. M. C. was charged with a wonderful unpretentious energy of making poetry and poetic community out of whatever and whoever she found. We kept in touch after we both left Minneapolis, and when in summer 2021 she offered an online poetry class with Ashna Ali, I jumped at it. Through that class I met Elsbeth Pancrazi, whose long-distance writing partnership was essential in finishing this book.

Thanks to my friends, colleagues, and family, including Alexandra de Havilland, Alyssa Noble, Andrea Applebee, Angie Crews, Ben Siems, Brian Howe, Chris Fischbach, Chris Vitiello, Cindra Halm, Corinne Duchesne, Danielle Brestel; the queen of "and," Glenda Lee; my more-than-neighbors, Hal and Anne Bogerd; Haley Lasché, Heidi Farrah, Jessica Q. Stark, Justin Tornow, Kylie Snyder, Lara Mimosa Montes, Laura Ritchie, Leah Wilks, Linda Shapiro, Marjie Laizure, Meaghan Mulholland, Michael Kliën (Christina, Rosa, Salome), Nicola Bullock, Sarah Fox; Sarah Mine, Sarah Rose Nordgren (through whom I joined a climate and parenting group led by Elizabeth Blechard, where I met Lilly Hankins, who has been an invaluable listening partner); Sarah Weissberg (Ben, Eliot), Stefania Heim, Susan Kincaid, Susan Meyers, Suzanne Wiltgen (Kelly, Nicolina, Julius); Trudy Hale, host of The Porches; and Vera Luck.

Thanks to everyone at Coffee House past and present, including Anitra Budd, Lizzie Davis, Daley Farr, Zoë Koenig, Abbie Phelps, Courtney Rust, and Marit Swanson. It is amazing to be held in your collective energy.

Many thanks to the journals in which some of these poems were first published, including *Concision Poetry Journal, Bennington Review, Potomac Review,* and *Pleiades.*

Thanks to Erika Stevens, who saw this work through its last twists and turns.

I started my newsletter *now**ing in January 2020, and its readers, drawn from all sides of my life, sustain my faith in the difficult mission of being a whole and authentic person in community. Thanks to you all, and to Nancy Hillsman *in memoriam.*

Thanks to Jack and Leigh and of course to Joseph, who daily makes me possible.

Oberon, how I miss you, my king of cats!

To my mother, love, because that is what I find at the bottom of the box.

Coffee House Press began as a small letterpress operation in 1972 and has grown into an internationally renowned nonprofit publisher of literary fiction, essay, poetry, and other work that doesn't fit neatly into genre categories.

Coffee House is both a publisher and an arts organization. Through our *Books in Action* program and publications, we've become interdisciplinary collaborators and incubators for new work and audience experiences. Our vision for the future is one where a publisher is a catalyst and connector.

LITERATURE
is not the same thing as
PUBLISHING

Funder Acknowledgments

Coffee House Press is an internationally renowned independent book publisher and arts nonprofit based in Minneapolis, MN; through its literary publications and *Books in Action* program, Coffee House acts as a catalyst and connector—between authors and readers, ideas and resources, creativity and community, inspiration and action.

Coffee House Press books are made possible through the generous support of grants and donations from corporations, state and federal grant programs, family foundations, and the many individuals who believe in the transformational power of literature. This activity is made possible by the voters of Minnesota through a Minnesota State Arts Board Operating Support grant, thanks to the legislative appropriation from the Arts and Cultural Heritage Fund. Coffee House also receives major operating support from the Amazon Literary Partnership, Jerome Foundation, Literary Arts Emergency Fund, McKnight Foundation, and the National Endowment for the Arts (NEA). To find out more about how NEA grants impact individuals and communities, visit www.arts.gov.

Coffee House Press receives additional support from Bookmobile; Dorsey & Whitney LLP; Elmer L. & Eleanor J. Andersen Foundation; the Gaea Foundation; the Matching Grant Program Fund of the Minneapolis Foundation; Mr. Pancks' Fund in memory of Graham Kimpton; the Schwab Charitable Fund; and the U.S. Bank Foundation.

The Publisher's Circle of Coffee House Press

Publisher's Circle members make significant contributions to Coffee House Press's annual giving campaign. Understanding that a strong financial base is necessary for the press to meet the challenges and opportunities that arise each year, this group plays a crucial part in the success of Coffee House's mission.

Recent Publisher's Circle members include many anonymous donors, Patricia A. Beithon, Anitra Budd, Andrew Brantingham, Kelli & Dave Cloutier, Mary Ebert & Paul Stembler, Kamilah Foreman, Eva Galiber, Jocelyn Hale & Glenn Miller Charitable Fund of the Minneapolis Foundation, the Rehael Fund-Roger Hale/ Nor Hall of the Minneapolis Foundation, Randy Hartten & Ron Lotz, Dylan Hicks & Nina Hale, William Hardacker, Kenneth & Susan Kahn, the Kenneth Koch Literary Estate, Cinda Kornblum, Jennifer Kwon Dobbs & Stefan Liess, the Lenfestey Family Foundation, Rebecca Rand, Sarah Lutman & Rob Rudolph, the Carol & Aaron Mack Charitable Fund of the Minneapolis Foundation, Gillian McCain, Mary & Malcolm McDermid, Robin Chemers Neustein, Daniel N. Smith III & Maureen Millea Smith, Enrique & Jennifer Olivarez, Robin Preble, Nan G. Swid, Grant Wood, and Margaret Wurtele.

For more information about the Publisher's Circle and other ways
to support Coffee House Press books, authors, and activities,
please visit www.coffeehousepress.org/pages/donate
or contact us at info@coffeehousepress.org.

LIGHTSEY DARST has published three previous books of poetry with Coffee House Press, including *Find the Girl*, which was awarded a Minnesota Book Award for Poetry. She is the recipient of two National Endowment for the Arts fellowships, one for dance criticism and one for poetry. She lives in Durham, North Carolina, with her family.

The Heiress/Ghost Acres was designed by
Bookmobile Design & Digital Publisher Services.
Text is set in Adobe Garamond Pro.